I Call to You from Time

I Call to You from Time

JUDITH SORNBERGER

RESOURCE *Publications* · Eugene, Oregon

I CALL TO YOU FROM TIME

Copyright © 2019 Judith Sornberger. All rights reserved. Except for brief quotations in critical publications or reviews, no part of this book may be reproduced in any manner without prior written permission from the publisher. Write: Permissions, Wipf and Stock Publishers, 199 W. 8th Ave., Suite 3, Eugene, OR 97401.

Resource Publications
An Imprint of Wipf and Stock Publishers
199 W. 8th Ave., Suite 3
Eugene, OR 97401

www.wipfandstock.com

PAPERBACK ISBN: 978-1-5326-8809-6
HARDCOVER ISBN: 978-1-5326-8810-2
EBOOK ISBN: 978-1-5326-8811-9

Manufactured in the U.S.A.   MAY 16, 2019

This book is dedicated to my sons
Jamie Emerson Sornberger
and Matthew Todd Sornberger,
who gave me the sacred gift of motherhood,

and to my mother
Roberta Ann McCord Mickel
my first model of mothering

Contents

Acknowledgments / ix

Frontispiece:
Inside-Out Pantoum / 1

I. / 3

Why I Am Not Quite a Buddhist / 5
The Gulf / 6
Antiphon / 8
Attempting Meditation / 10
Vermeer's Lacemaker / 11
What I Heard This Morning Filling the Birdfeeder / 13
Never Mine / 15
With My Mother in the Garden / 16
Facing It / 18
So Many Blues / 20
Believing in Bats / 22
Asking for Ancient Paths / 23

II. / 25

Annunciation / 27
The Holy Ghost Shows Up at Tai Chi Class / 29
Mary, After the Angel / 30
Prayer of Thread and Needle / 31
The Mother of Grown Twins at the Gallery / 33

Mary Muses on the Missing Portrait / 35
Mary Ponders the Nature of Free Will / 37
December 26 / 39
Just this Once, Just this Much / 41
As It Is in Heaven / 42

III. / 45

Flight into Egypt / 47
Prayer as Tanks Slouch toward Baghdad / 48
Invocation in February / 50
Madonna of the Wheat / 52
Prayer for a Two-year-old Boy Whose Father Is at War / 53
Hawk / 55
The Wal-Mart in Tioga County / 57
City and State, Please / 60
Madonna of the Disappeared / 62
Prayer on Candlemas / 64
Our Lady of Guadalupe Appears to Me at Wal-Mart / 65
Why Is There So Much Sadness in Your Poems? / 67

IV. / 69

Abstract Arc / 71
Protest / 73
Van Gogh's Pieta / 75
The Way to Forgiveness / 77
I Call to You from Time / 79
If She Could / 80
Our Lady Releasing Her Sorrow / 81
Echo, Late Winter / 82

Rebirth / 83
Lenten Practice as the Climate Changes / 85
Grace / 86
Screen Saver / 87
Our Lady of the Rest Stop / 89
Prayer Flags / 91
Junction / 93

Acknowledgments

I WISH TO THANK the following periodicals and anthologies in which these poems first appeared:

50/50: Poems & Translations by Womxn over 50: "Just this Once, Just this Much," edited by Ann Davenport, Quills Edge Press

Calyx: "Protest" and "What I Heard this Morning Filling the Birdfeeder"

Encore: More Poems by Parallel Press Poets: "Prayer Flags," Parallel Press

Feminist Studies: "Our Lady of Guadalupe Appears to Me at Wal-Mart" and "The Wal-Mart in Tioga County"

Hawaii Pacific Review: "Why I Am Not a Buddhist"

Hidden Manna: "Annunciation" and "Mary Ponders the Nature of Free Will"

Nebraska Humanities: "Hawk"

Out of Line: Imaginative Writings on Peace and Justice: "Prayer as Tanks Slouch Toward Baghdad," edited by Sam Longmire, Garden House Press

Pilgrimage: "Antiphon"

Acknowledgments

Poems & Plays: "Mary, after the Angel" and "If She Could"

Potpourri: "Van Gogh's *Pieta*"

Prairie Schooner: "Vermeer's Lacemaker"

White Pelican Review: "Our Lady of the Rest Stop"

Windhover: "Lenten Practice"

The following poems appeared in the chapbook *Bones of Light* (Parallel Press):

"Hawk," "The Gulf," "If She Could," and "Van Gogh's *Pieta*"

The poems below appeared in *The Hard Grammar of Gratitude*, winner of the Tennessee Chapbook Contest, published as an internal chapbook in *Poems & Plays*:

"Inside-out Pantoum," "December 26," "Rebirth," "Junction" and "Why I Am Not a Buddhist"

The poems below were published in the chapbook *Wal-Mart Orchid*, winner of the Helen Kay Award (Evening Street Press):

"Antiphon," "Prayer Flags," "Our Lady of Guadalupe Appears to Me at Wal-Mart," "Protest" "City and State, Please," and "The Wal-Mart in Tioga County"

I am grateful to The Ucross Foundation and Norcroft for writing residencies during which some of these poems were written.

ACKNOWLEDGMENTS

Gratitude also to Mansfield University of Pennsylvania for a sabbatical during which some of these poems were written.

Thanks to my late husband Bruce Barton for thirty years of sharing a writing life; to my anam cara and writing partner Alison Townsend for her support, comments, and encouragement; to Lilace Mellin Guignard for friendship and laughter, our writing residencies together, and for her help with many of these poems; to Mary Ginn for the inspiration of her friendship; to my sister Jill Mickel for our many talks about creativity; to Walter Sanders, David Steinbeck, and Tom Murphy for their insights on some of these poems; and to Karl Schneider, my life partner and my love.

Inside-Out Pantoum

Prayer is a there
I often cannot enter.
However much I haunt the grounds,
pace around its stucco-washed façade,

strain my gaze through sainted glass,
prayer is a there
whose door is locked, whose incense
I too often cannot enter.

I shake the oak door in its jamb,
strain my gaze through sainted glass,
but cannot enter the within
whose door is locked, whose incense

will not enter my blood's chambers.
I shake the oak door in its jamb,
as if it is no part of who I am,
but I cannot enter the within.

Or prayer is an element so foreign
I won't invite it into my blood's chambers,
an inner sea I fear to drown in
as if it is no part of who I am.

As if it is a where I can dive into,
prayer is an element so foreign
I hold my breath to enter
the inner sea I fear to drown in.

Prayer ripples and gleams darkly
as if it is a where I can dive into,
a depth I stroke against
even as I hold my breath to enter,

still holding to a vision of myself
in prayer's ripples gleaming darkly.
Sometimes the inner sea sends up a swell,
a depth I stroke against.

I am not allowed to enter there
still holding to a vision of myself.
Still, when the inner sea sends up its swell,
sometimes I am mercifully swallowed.

I.

Why I Am Not Quite a Buddhist

God has many eyes
in the bark of the birch.
Not one blinks as I walk past
or winces at what wafts
through my mind's branches.

Each eye is wide, solemn
as the eye of the doe tonight
holding me in her sights
as I wash lettuce leaves
before the window and she nips
seeds from the birdfeeder.

When she tiptoes off with half
the birds' booty in her belly,
the sky in me widens like laughter,
bristles with stars, each an eye
opening wide as it can, ravenous
for this world's bounty.

The Gulf

Each night when I was eight
I lay me down to pray:
Bless Mom and Dad and Jen and Jill,
bless Mona and Granddad, bless . . .
Oh, the list would bore you.
And each night the arms of my prayer
reached farther and farther beyond the cave
of covers, past our house, our city, our country . . .
Everything, even the stars, needed my blessing.

My parents were watching the news
when I called out: *In a few minutes
tell me to stop saying my prayers.*
My fervor frightened them.
Now there is a term for it:
obsessive-compulsive disorder.
But it was order I believed in,
and I was at its center.

Then one day without warning
the fever of my faith broke,
and I was cured. I was grown
and had a life like many others:
husband, job, two children.
And I knew how not to pray.

But tonight on the news there is war:
a broken face I can't stand to see.
A POW—a pilot—his shoulders
folded in like ruined wings.

There is an enemy. There must be.
They are his torturers.
Or they are my leaders.
Or it is the camera—an eye like God's
that sees pain and accepts it

Of one thing I am certain:
this man suffers for our sins—
but which ones: omission or commission?
Obsession or compulsion? There must be
some disorder we can name it, and some cure
for how we lay us down, for how we sleep.

Antiphon

On the way to the monastery I get pissed
at a guy parked too long at the pump
while I wait to fill my tank. I see him
inside laughing with his girlfriend
and the cashier, purchasing lottery tickets,
which, I guess, is his form of prayer.
But I don't care. My motor is running
and he's in my way. I have to get prayed
in by the guest porter by 4:30
or I'll miss supper and Vespers.

I don't yell or anything, but how
is he supposed to answer when I criticize
his lack of courtesy? *Fuck you, you bitch,*
he says, grabbing his crotch, to which
I respond by flipping him the bird
as I roar off, heart beating like wings,
pondering the way a simple case of being late
fueled by impatience can flare into a conflagration.
And wondering how, in just 45 minutes,
I can be transfigured, become a woman
worthy of the Psalms.

I make it there in time, though my heart
is still revving in my chest as the cantor leads
us in chanting one of those psalms asking
God to smite our wicked foes,
exulting that God's victory is ours.

Ordinarily, I squirm through such words,
not wanting to add my voice to them,
but now I sing, *Let the mischief of their lips
overwhelm them! Let burning coals fall on them,*
stifling a giggle in the shame of recognition.
Who isn't more at home in this setting
with the sentiments that follow: *Too long
I have had my dwelling among those
who hate peace. I am for peace.*

The psalmist's schizophrenia has always made
me crazy, until today when I hear the words
echoing each tone of my soul, see my
ugliness and beauty mirrored there,
asking along with everyone around me:
*If you, O Lord, mark iniquities,
who would be left standing?*

Attempting Meditation

First, I inhale: *May I be . . .*
Then the exhale: *one with You.*
I have no idea what this means.

Thoughts flurry like birds come to feed.
Seed's tempting, and I chew.
Now back to inhale: May I be

sap pulsing through a sleeping tree
a toddler's crayon drew.
I'm not to imagine what this means.

Not supposed to think or dream.
Not supposed to move.
Just to inhale. May I be

a fallen leaf riding the stream
that lulls me toward Your womb.
Why can't imagination be the means?

Metaphor's the way I breathe,
how I follow Your tune.
When I inhale, may I be
listening for all You mean.

Vermeer's Lacemaker

There never is much light
in these enclosures.
Nor do eyes rise
to spark a reflection.

The light requires
an eyelid, cheek, lace
collar as palette.

As thread relies on
the sharp eye, the minuet
of fingers, pins and bobbins.

She doesn't know
how small she is—
one of his tiny canvasses—
or that she is detained,
held still as a fly
in the dried paint.

If she tried to stretch
her arms or stand,
she might flutter
into a tarantella,
batter her composure.

Patient as a spider,
she works light
into pattern, draws
from her dark interior
the single strand
of her attention.

What I Heard This Morning Filling the Birdfeeder

You thought I said *dominion*?
Oh dear. Let's backtrack
here a little. As each bird
flew from my fingers,
each whale and finny thing
swam from my tongue,
each beast of the earth
crept into being, I remember
quite distinctly saying,
Welcome to your domus.
They all seemed to get it
and set out to find their rooms.

I greeted you with the same words.
Could it be that you misheard?
Or were you already
too big for your fig leaves?
Or did the error come
when I whispered your mission?
That's always the trouble
with translation. Listen,
If I'd made one creature
king, wouldn't I at least
have installed wings?

If I'd meant you to go on
this way, would I have tossed
wings down the dark avenue
of early morning to wait
in the arbor vitae for you,
putting on, one by one,
their sparrow voices:
Wake up. Wake up.
Wake up.

Never Mine

No more sermons on this mountain as I climb,
not even the internal kind, calling down
fire and brimstone on gas drillers
and their belching trucks who, in one day,
stomp a course through fir and birch
broad enough for legions.

Today I will return to the seminary
of pine scent, lift my face for snowflakes
to anoint, trace the narrow way etched
by millennia of deer hooves following
a righteous hunger, track the silence
left behind, sacred epistle—
quotation marks pressed into the snow,
no words between them.

With My Mother in the Garden

*from the Polish Madonna oil paintings
of Wislawa Kwiatkowska*

Though you weren't into Mary,
you'd love these woodsy princesses
with long hair like your daughters'
when we were still your girls.
Whom do these girls belong to
with their peacock feather dresses,
cranberry-studded crowns,
bare feet even in winter?
To women like us, of course,
whose gardens are their chapels.

Mary's train is an entourage
of deer and bear and cougar,
and a flurry of herons, finches,
sparrows rise from the breeze
of her cape as she makes her way
between chrysanthemum and lily—
the simultaneous bursting
forth of seasons—in a garden
eternity has never fled.

It's the kind of place where
I'm always looking for you, sure
when you appear to one of us,
it will be where fur and petals,
wings and leaves are
always weaving this world
from the next one.

Facing It

How many poets does it take to change the world?
All the elegies ever written for creatures
killed on roads can't bring back a single one.

Today I still live in the world where goldfinches gorge
on dandelion fluff in morning sun. When I open
the window they still rise in multitudes—a fountain
bright, I tell myself, as forgiveness.

Yesterday, driving faster than anyone needs to,
I felt a bump, a loud clunk against my tire.
In the mirror, the snapping turtle rocked in the highway
on its carapace. She must have been crossing
on her way to lay eggs.

I could have turned around several times, but why go back?
It was late, and there might be worse to see than claws
raking the air. But, finally, I did what people sometimes do—
turned around to face the damage.

Though other cars had passed, they must have swerved,
for she lay as I'd left her. One leg trembled
when I picked her up, and scarlet drops dripped from her beak.

I set her in deep grass well off the asphalt, pretending, I suppose,
that she might make it to wherever she was going to bury
her leathery globes. What do other people do after they see

what they've destroyed? What do they do if they don't write poems?

How many snappers crossing the road does it take for a nest of eggs
to hatch, for a single hatchling to scramble to water
before it's munched by snake, raccoon or skunk?

What will it take for the world to keep crawling forward,
scraping its egg-laden belly, toward a place
ancient as the dream of going on?

So Many Blues

in this year's version of November.
If I counted the hues of each day—
each moment floating by—
would that too be prayer? I try
to read the open face of morning—
nothing to mar it but whatever I say,
however I move. Even my breath
could cloud it. Is that why
I am afraid to pray?

Because I can't be fearless
as the morning, or the first dove
to flutter through it? Does she know
what she is daring? But You are more
than canopy, deeper than backdrop.
Maybe more than light—

our favorite metaphor for how
You fill us. After all, how do
sea creatures beneath the press
of darkness fathom You?
Are they, perhaps, the true
experts of faith? Not the birds
who are almost angels, not us
with all the words we use

to prop the cosmos open,
to see, we hope, inside You.
When we are closest in deep
twilight when longing surges
from our depths and pulls
us under and we wish
that we were creatures
who could breathe You.

Believing in Bats

for my ten-year-old friend Gloria

In moments, they'll dissolve into the dark,
replaced by stars, but we happen to step
just in time into the late dusk of early Fall.
Look, Glo, bats! I say as first one, then another
and another flit across our vision like black comets or—
if this were a fairy tale—some witch's minions.
Real bats? she whispers in the tone of wonder
once reserved for fairies. *I only saw them once
on a field trip in a cave where they were sleeping.*
And I imagine them, folded up like last year's
lawn chairs stored over the winter.

She's with me while her dad has surgery to see
if cancer's spreading. She's known only one other
person with cancer—my husband who she loved,
still talking of the night he twirled her round and round
our living room during the *Barbie Nutcracker*
when she was five, a year before he died.

You're so lucky to have bats in your yard, she says.
I know. I don't tell her 99% of our state's bats
have vanished from white nose syndrome
while scientists work overtime to bring them back.
Tonight, I take the dance of myriad wings
as miracle, ignore the way they look like tattered
black kid gloves waving goodbye.

Asking for Ancient Paths

*Stand at the crossroads and look,
and ask for ancient paths.*

JEREMIAH 6:16

Behind the home where I hope to die
I bow beneath a low colonnade
of snow-bent branches,
entering the ascent I love
bent over like the monk
at the monastery I visit
whose body can no longer straighten
because—I prefer to believe—
of the long habit of bowing.

That's how I spot the deep stitches
of deer prints I am careful
not to smother with my boots.
Then a chickadee swoops out
from nowhere, looping its bright
flight from bough to bough,
and I envision following it
straight to the blue summit.

Then my gaze snags on a branch
tied with orange plastic,
and there ahead's another,
and soon I'm following
these obscene streamers

so I don't see where
deer tracks disappear
beneath the gouge of tires.

Now it's not the climb
turning my breath jagged,
but reading the portents—
gas drilling has arrived even here,
trampling the sacred in its path.

Like the other creatures
all around me,
I am standing
at the crossroads,
God, and looking.

II.

Annunciation

from the fresco by Fra Angelico in the Cloister of San Marco

All over Florence angels make announcements
they have made for centuries to Mary's
holding poses no one would believe.
But, finally, I find you here—
as the angel found you—slumped on a stool,
pulling into the cave of yourself, hands
crossing: two wings over your belly.
You don't have your finger in a book,
pretending nonchalance when he shows up
in gold-embroidered robes and wings
still dripping rainbows.

Not like those staged rendezvous:
Gabriel bowing suitor-like,
offering his nosegay of white lilies;
Mary a coy courtesan decked out
in her best dress and diadem, knees
saying no-no as they sashay
away from his honeyed words,
torso swaying into his advances.

It's not his rosy finery
I can't turn away from.
It's the stunned yes
of your face I recognize.
I have sat as you do in this portico,

knowing I could answer yes or no.
And I have passed through the pillars
of this archway, praising the great
wisdom of the body.

Oh, but how I envy you this moment:
knowing the world will never be the same,
still innocent of how your world will change.

The Holy Ghost Shows Up at Tai Chi Class

I wasn't expecting her.
She hadn't registered,
and I didn't see her slip in
as we warmed up—*opening from within;*
pulling down the sky; pressing heaven/
pressing earth. Perhaps She read
our movements as an invocation,
especially during *stand like a tree*
while we sank roots from our soles
into the earth—arms out like trunks
before us. Maybe that's when she
entered us, rising up our xylem.
Maybe she is what we mean by *Chi.*
As we *paint the rainbow*, I notice
the glow she strokes across our faces.
And when we fold, then widen, our arms,
becoming the *wild dove spreading its wings,*
I feel her soaring through us like the dove
flying between God and the Virgin
in paintings of the Annunciation—
our guide between body and spirit.

Mary, After the Angel

*from Transformations:
Looking to the Future with Dove,*
EGG TEMPERA ON PANEL, 10 X 8 INCHES,
BY CAROL COTHNER

What has he left her
but this puzzled profile,
these arms wooden

with wonder, this window
that holds neither
moon nor star,

this dove she pulls
into her girlish midriff,
hands crossed like waiting

wings across its breast,
cradling the fierce
pulse of the future.

Prayer of Thread and Needle

for Nancy

This is what you have a pattern for:
this suit and cap, size newborn,
cut from cloth the very blue
the sky should be over
every new and perfect creature.
Feel how soft, you offer
and we press it to our faces.

Except this week your daughter's
ultrasound revealed a bubble
on her baby's brain. And all
I can do is sew beside you
at my dining room table, boil water
for tea, put on the season's first carols.

The fluted lullabies of ages
stitch us to a story whose ending
no mother should have to ponder
in this season of the fetus.

You keep worrying
that you've done something wrong
sewing the tiny cap.
Where did these puckers come from?
You pull and fluff, smooth and adjust.
I've never seen you, my sewing mentor—

goddess of the straight seam
and whipper-upper of everything
from witches' capes to kitchen curtains—
so uncertain.

But when it comes to my doll-sized coverlet
you know just what to do to turn it
right side out once I've stuffed
the thing and sewn the edges shut.
It's called birthing the quilt, you announce,
rolling from the farthest corner
until you've got an infant-sized bundle
to draw through the short slit
you'd told me to leave open.

It seems nearly impossible,
but you tuck and pull with the cool
patience of a midwife until
this one slice of the universe
slides clear—beautiful and whole—
the way we planned it.

The Mother of Grown Twins at the Gallery

I keep trying to pull away
from the small window
of one painting: two eggs, a nest.
That's it. I guess the perspective
is what gets me: from above,
as though I am the mother leaving
or returning. Or just pulling
a lighter version of herself
into air to glimpse the shape
of what she is protecting.
Of course, there is no mother
in the painting.

I wander off and try
to like abstract things,
knowing I should curb
my taste for the familiar,
my nostalgia for the things
of this world. I'm a grown-up
woman, and I should admire
color for its own sake—whole skies
of red without a metaphor in sight—
not want it to congeal
into an apple, corpse, or tulip.

Why do I keep trying to make
every sphere into a planet,
peering into every oval
for a trace of features?

And returning to this tiny room
of light and color—this woven womb,
these sealed and speckled chambers.
It's all I can do not to break
the rules and curl my palms
around them. Or keep watch
until she swoops back into view.

Mary Muses on the Missing Portrait

A pregnant woman
understands Eternity—
never quite believes
the days of dreaming her child
into breath will end.
Until they do.

My child was baptized first
in his mother's waters.
I hold it still
the holiest of washings.
They say I felt no pain
when my body split,
that I remained unbroken.

Where were those Fathers
when I told Joseph
stop the donkey now,
water spilling between
my legs: a revelation.

Where are the portraits
of that moment?
Giotto, Rembrandt, Titian—
you with all your genius
couldn't see it.

Not even Artemisia,
both mother and painter,
caught me falling to my knees
in hunched wonder.
Even she would not deliver
my writhing to the canvas:
the second when I knew
the angel had been true.

What else but God's arrival
could occasion such a starburst
of brute straining? Why has no one
painted that epiphany across my vision?

Mary Ponders the Nature of Free Will

after *Madonna with Child* by Fra Filippo Lippi

Your hands know nothing
but tenderness, yet your eyes
slide away from the child
on your lap picking each bead
of blood from the pomegranate
resting in your palm.

Brows arch above your hooded eyes
like wings that would fly
to another story. Old eyes,
these, in such a lineless face.
Eyes that know what's going on
behind your back, behind the whirring
blade of your halo.

It's like a little factory back there:
Reach back and up and you can almost
touch your mother propped against
her pillows after childbirth,
handing your swaddled body to a servant,
her fingers reluctant to leave
the blonde fur of your cheek,
as though they fear the fate
they give you to.

A few steps farther back and up,
she greets your father, pulls him
upstairs through the doorway
of the room where she'll conceive you.

Do you wonder, my dear,
when the angel came to your door
that ordinary morning, if, eons before,
he had squinted through the keyhole
of this split-level story, glimpsing
this trinity of scenes?
Were you already seated
in the foreground of this tondo
before he knelt, wings throbbing
in the charged air between you?
Before he called you lucky girl
and reached into the perfect, pressed
folds of his robe to release the white bird?
Pages and pages before you whispered,
Let it be so.

December 26

from *Christmas Madonna*,
a Christmas card painting by Edward Hays

Mary, you look anything but merry
beneath your circlet of barbed holly,
even though you're the picture of plenty—
pears and pomegranates spilling
between your knees, a gleaming ring
of keys braceleting one wrist
to open the kingdom or the pantry.

One arm cradling a decked out, glowing fir,
the other circling the child who occasioned
all this fuss, this mess—the over-
flowing box of baubles at your feet
beside the dripping bowl of cookie dough,
the greeting cards yet to be addressed,
the mandolin and score of *Silent Night*
for the caroling you've yet to organize.

I suppose you imagined your *yes*
was a once in a lifetime deal,
never guessed you'd birth this monster
of a season, dooming and—yes, blessing, too—
the women of your line to heavy labor.
I admit each year I buy it, too,
fall for the glittering angel's seduction,
for silent babies, stars and cozy mangers
on the cards I truly mean to send.

Amnesia veils my head and shoulders
like a snowy mantle, like the one
falling on women after they deliver
so we will go on falling on our knees
in fresh wonder, saying *yes* and *yes*
and *yes*, till we find ourselves one morning
gazing off into the distance, stone-faced
with exhaustion, blinking our eyes, frantic
to get out from under all this favor.

Just this Once, Just this Much

a Zen saying

The homeless shelter asked if I'd drive you to register your kids for school. I offered to buy us breakfast biscuits at Dunkin Donuts first. Your teenage son helped the little ones with drinks and straws. Once we'd finished eating, you asked if I would take a look at your staples. You'd had back surgery just days before. Someone needed to check for signs of infection. *I could have done that, Ma*, your son said. You ignored him. I'm sorry. I don't remember his name or yours. *Watch the kids,* she told him as we left the table. The tiny bathroom stank of human waste, and the sink was dirty. You straddled the toilet backward and pulled up the back of your sweatshirt. Like a giant zipper, the staples climbed your back from waist nearly to neck. How simply some wounds are mended. No redness, no swelling. We were done. I wanted to hold you. I wanted to run.

As It Is in Heaven

for Susan Williams Beckhorn

Going to church, my friend calls
her Sunday forest rambles.
Yet glimpsing my Nativity last Christmas,
Sue admitted craving one.
I savor such paradoxes—mysteries
like Jesus being *fully God and fully man*.

So when I happen on the Holy Family
and their entourage huddled between
die-cast soldiers and Kewpie dolls
at a roadside antiques mall a week
before Sue's solstice party, I don't know
what to call it—luck or grace.

Especially when I see the price
on a tag that also reads *as is*.
Searching for flaws, I caress
their silky porcelain contours,
discover the donkey's broken back,
inexpertly repaired, and one
Wise Man missing a thumb.

But I know she'll cherish
the sweet wonder of their faces
and forgive the imperfections
in this unlikely congregation of shepherds,
angels, kings, and barnyard beasts.

Like us around Sue's table, mostly unbelievers—
potters, bus drivers, professors, contractors,
divorced, disabled, and widowed—
finished with our turkey and watching her
unwrap each tissue-swaddled figure,
her fingers tender as when undressing
her babes before their baths deep in the past.

Oh, our murmurs and delighted sighs—
like children, starry-eyed, watching a pageant—
as she sets each one beside the others,

once again collapsing time to tell their story,
the one in which we're all *as is* and, in this moment
of shared awe, perfectly mended.

III.

Flight into Egypt

from the *Scenes from Life of Christ* cycle
painted for the doors of a silver chest by Fra Angelico

This child is no symbol dropped from stars
into your lap, no accessory to your perfection.
So you don't let his nimbus prevent your
pressing his smooth cheek into your own,
folding his warmth back into your body.

You, your baby, and the donkey are the three-in-one
of this journey, bobbing along in a single rhythm.
Poor Joseph might as well be out of the picture,
skulking along behind—a supernumerary.

Can the clop of hooves disguise the march of soldiers
in the next scene? Does crooning to your infant close
your eyes, keep you innocent of mothers shrieking,
the gurgling of blood from tiny throats? *Stop!*
I want to scream: this path will lead you into the melee.

In the dreamy mist of rising dust,
I try to see you riding off
the map of history and myth, delivering your son
from prophets' tongues, not sticking
to the plot you didn't author.

Prayer as Tanks Slouch toward Baghdad

A refugee from CNN tonight,
I seek sanctuary in this monster
bookstore that has swallowed
whole so many smaller ones.
Yet, as Jonah did,
many a story lives on
in its belly.

I am here because the war
has swallowed my son,
and touching paper is the next
best thing to touching skin.

Hear my prayer for human skin—
the one I write across this hand-
made paper, my felt tip stumbling
across crushed flowers.

Beside me a blonde girl caresses
the contours of her cappuccino
as a dreadlocked boy tells her
of the Nile—his voice ancient
with wonder. I pray for the tender
petals of fingertips—hers
that I can almost feel burning

to cross the distance to his face,
their voices flowing

me into other rivers—the Tigris
and Euphrates whose names reporters
invoke every broadcast, names

I never heard till seventh
grade, in a room on a flat prairie
cradled by two other rivers,
Mrs. Wiltse's voice crooning
cradle of civilization and my writing
the words because I liked
the way they sounded.

I'm praying now for a body
I imagine in a distant cradle,
for arms that lift and carry it,
folded close, under stars toward
the river that inscribes the border
between that place and hope.
For the crazy quilt of skin
covering this planet.

Invocation in February

It's true that I am grateful
for the snow, for soft, deep banks
I drift beneath in sleep.
Even in daylight, I would hide
from you there—from You
and the world You made,
where wings fly my son to war
without my permission
or collusion.

I would never say yes,
no matter how You phrased it,
no matter what You threatened.
Never sharpen my knife
for his throat. Never
hand him over without a fight.

I do not know
what will be asked of me.
But this morning I am walking
through snowfall where a jay
is revealed in the Y
of a tree, blowing her blue
notes into the sky.

What gets me is the way
it takes her whole body lifting—

how she goes up on her tiptoes—
to launch her tune toward You.
And how I ride those brief notes
suddenly into Your presence.

Madonna of the Wheat

from the painting by Wislawa Kwiatkowska

I like Jesus better
when he's a helpless baby in your arms,
not this miniature dandy
in a red dress trimmed in gold,
arms outstretched as though
he would fly from you already.

Or does he extend his arms to bless
the field mice poised impossibly
on strands of golden wheat, front feet
waving hosannas, in this frame
where rodents replace angels?

Or he is a tiny host
spreading his arms in welcome,
bidding us partake of sheaves
climbing the sky, weaving
a veil between the dead and living.

Your russet hair reaches down
to enclose his halo. Your fingers
meeting at his waist are folded wings,
are praying. You must know
there is a seed ticking within him,
that there will be a harvest
and a grinding.

Prayer for a Two-year-old Boy Whose Father Is at War

I could tell You he fell
from Your tree into our arms
in the gold month we call October.
That the name he calls me—*Abuelita*—
comes from his mother's first tongue.

When he is too tired to sleep,
sometimes he whimpers
Daddy?
I could tell You
that this is his prayer.

I wish I knew the language
to explain *porque*
Daddy *no esta en casa.*

No.

Let there never be words
in any tongue
to make sense
of such an absence.
Let language that attempts it
be found guilty of treason,
to the love that is his birthright.

Let it perish beside other phrases
that can never tell the truth,
like *collateral damage,*
friendly fire,
acceptable losses.

Hawk

I've never looked so long
at the underside of a thing,
never had that luxury—
that soaring above me in a circle
as if my eyes were prey
or its beloved.
Never held to my eyes
lenses for marks that tell
one species from another,
never knew anything without a doubt:
the white windows on wings,
the slivered, white cross of the body,
the dark V where the legs are
soldered on—a positive i.d.:
ferruginous hawk.

So different from the red-tailed
whose name lies as often
as it tells the truth.
Sometimes hawks don't follow
the rules of our books.
The rule of my heart is to love
before I can identify the source.
It's a risk like prairie dogs
standing in full relief against
the blue October, the risk they take
by living in the open.

I've come here to learn to tell
one love from another, to locate
the muscles of vision, the tight
enough squint, to find the patience.
Is it patience or hypnosis
that holds the prairie dog
to the hawk's circle, the hawk's
naming the rodent in its slow
language of ever smaller circles: *prey*
> *prey*
>> *prey*

The Wal-Mart in Tioga County

The checkout is a sort of Pearly Gates
where desire is weighed against limitation.
Behind me waits a couple that looks
too old to be the parents of the small
children in their care.

The girl—three, maybe—wanders
to where I stand, pulls herself up
to the counter, watching my things
slide by. *Shenai!* the woman growls.
The girl ignores her. *Shenai!*
she roars this time,
and I am cringing, but still
the girl won't hear her.

The woman lunges, grabs her
wrist and yanks her like a rag
doll through the air.
When Shenai cries her brother
hugs and tries to soothe her,
keeping one eye on the woman.

*I don't think you realize
that you could really hurt her
that way,* says some know-it-all
bitch from up at the college
with her beauty shop blonde bob
and outfit that will never
sell at Wal-Mart.

It ain't your business, lady,
she snarls at me.
Behind her, the man backs up,
inch by inch,
with the cart and kids.
It is my business, I say,
returning the glare I'm certain
her husband wouldn't dare to.

Suddenly, she turns to him:
I can't take this. I can't!
she cries, hands gripping
the sides of her head.

He points her to the door
while he and the kids
move to another checkout.
But before she steps out, she turns:
You wanna take it outside, lady?

See? I want to say
to the checkout girl
whose eyebrows shot straight up
when I spoke out, then fell
back into the numb mask
they all wear here. *See
how crazy she is?*

But in the car my body trembles,
and I can't just back out
as if nothing's happened.
I have to sit there
for a moment, breathing.

As I drive away, the image
of the ragged face between
those red, torn hands
follows me home
where I can't shake
the feeling that it
is my business.

City and State, Please

Gang Mills, New York,
I think I'm saying to the voice
that never seems connected
to a person. A pause.
I know she's glued to
the blurred face of a computer,
but I imagine her thumbing
through a mammoth book
of all the places in the world
no one has heard of.

Gangville? she says.
*There's really a place
called Gangville?* I start to giggle.
No, it's Gang Mills.
Someplace in the United States
she cracks up, too, some spark
igniting between us, neither wanting
now to break the connection.
When our laughing fades to embers,
one of us fans it—*Gangville!*—
and it leaps back into flames again.

If only the brief campfire of our laughter
could call the disconnected kids
trying to find their way by knife-glint
through our cities, to create a tribe

and language out of gunshot and graffiti.
Sitting down, warming our hands,
we might recognize the same species
of need in one another as sparks lift
toward the stars, our oldest kin,
who never stop telling our stories.

Madonna of the Disappeared

for the *arpilleristas*: women of Chile and Peru who created
    the *arpilleras,* "tapestries that talk," textile records
    documenting the disappearance of nearly 160,000
    suspected political dissidents between 1970 and 1990

and for Fanny Arango-Keeth who showed me their work

Maria dear, why have you never appeared to the Mothers
of the Disappeared as they gathered in sad huddles
in church basements to stitch onto the vast canvas
of official silence the accusations that cannot be shut up?

Didn't you long to kiss blood from their hands?
Not the scarlet washed from inquisitors' fingers,
but the daily needle pricks of not knowing,
the small wounds acquired converting
absence to a substance tasted
by the eye and fondled—an illuminated
record of their version of the story
sewn from hope-bright scraps—stripes, paisleys,
and sock-you-in-the-eyeball solids.

Or did you, perhaps, sit on a folding chair
among them at the table, taking up a needle
to blanket stitch around *los hijos* being abducted?
Did you, for once, allow yourself to receive
the comfort—the camaraderie of tears and whispers?

Did you wonder if you were more fortunate
than they, allowed to witness muscle, breath
and tendon once stitched by your body
torn asunder, even if his corpse vanished
before you could anoint it?

Or are you, not he, the disappeared one—
summoned when a womb was needed,
then laid to rest until a mother's tears
were mandatory, but never allowed
to tell the story? Or if you told your version,
no scribe's hand recorded it as gospel.
Unless you count the hands creating *arpilleras.*

Prayer on Candlemas

Today how many candles must I light?
How many snowflakes in the wind's fierce fist?
How many upturned faces in the night?

Can suffering be soothed by such a rite?
Will anyone answer this flaming list?
Today how many candles must I light?

How can I rest knowing the sleepless plight
of widow, refugee, and terrorist—
so many upturned faces in the night?

How many stars flicker beyond our sight?
How many tears are falling in the mist?
Tonight how many candles must I light?

Can burning candles any hope ignite?
Will God descend as though to keep a tryst
with all our upturned faces in the night?

How much grace can one shaking hand invite?
Will ill befall if one candle is missed?
Today how many candles must I light?
How many upturned faces in the night?

Our Lady of Guadalupe Appears to Me at Wal-Mart

I'm flipping through teapot and teddy bear
toss pillows, when suddenly she's there,
floating before me in her fiery bubble,
feet resting on the crescent moon
as though it were her Universe canoe.

For just a tick I think she might be winking,
but it's only a wrinkle in the fabric
she is made of, and I marvel:
how did they make polyester and acrylic
look like weaving, like a page
from an illuminated Bible—all gold
and indigo and roses?

And how have they made me believe it?
How have I—Pagan-cum-Protestant—
come to hold this imported version
of the Virgin (whose label swears
she was *hecho en los Estados Unidos*)
to my breast, as though we belonged
to the same tribe, as though she were my
long lost mother who once tucked
the petal of her oldest name beneath my tongue.

As though carts weren't clattering past us
on their ways to Odor-Eaters, Tylenol,
and Love-that-Red lip gloss.
As though a voice overhead did not keep calling

a CSM to the Courtesy Counter.
As though I could follow her back
to some time before time, before
I became what I am:
part of this world
that discounts her.

Why Is There So Much Sadness in Your Poems?

Because sadness is a key unlocking many doors.
Because it sounds like the sweet whine
of a train whistle—backdrop to Dad's stories
of his cowboy days—and the cowboy songs
he taught us on the long drive west
through cattle-studded Sandhills where
the ranch was lost before I was born.

Because there's so much beauty
in songs composed in minor keys.
Because sadness feels like my mom's twisted
fingers, shaking as I stroked mother-
of-pearl polish over her ridged and nicotine-stained
nails a few weeks before she died.

Because sadness is a path to tenderness.
Because sadness looks like the student
in my poetry class who grew up in the ghetto,
his face melting back to boyhood
when he told of his mother saying Santa
didn't come because he was bad.

Because sadness is a gift delivered daily.
Because my son has never healed from
the glass breaking on our kitchen floor
when he was two, following the slamming

door after the fight between his parents,
a splinter shattering his vision in one eye. At 44,
he still anticipates the next wound and the next.

Because one sadness leads to another.
Because you may have had a mother,
a father, a son or a daughter,
Because you may have lost a home,
your vision, your belief in something.

Because sadness is the home where we're all kin.

IV.

Abstract Arc

> from the paintings of Mainie Jellett who brought
> the Modernist Art Movement to Ireland

When you expelled us from the garden of your canvas—
we watercolor nudes with ribboned hair, we girls reading
on beaches or twirling parasols over our shoulders,
we clouds and rocks and waves; when you named
each painting *Abstract Composition*
as if you must erase even our names—
*Betty on the Rocks, The Artist's Mother,
Woman in Summer Hat, The Blue Girl*—
to bring forth these jagged zones of color,
it looked like you were done with us forever.

But slowly you recalled us to those forms—
here a hint of human profile,
there a spiral-eyed, bronze bird or sun
hanging in what might be sky.
Until one day you called forth the waters
with arcs and lines and swirls
borrowed from your abstract worlds,
gave us your *Sea* fresh as the scent
of paint freshly applied, yet calling
to us in its ancient voice.

Then followed study after study
in pencil, crayon, gouache
for your *Abstract Crucifixion*,

and, finally, you gathered oils—
ochre, French blue, burnt siena—
to paint, at last, this hybrid—
this God-creature.

Here no scarlet trickles from a stricken face.
Your sunset-red halos a faceless head,
follows arms nailed to neither agony
nor glory, but spread out wide,
wing-like: an invitation.

Protest

I'm standing on the corner at the one light
in town with a band of boomers like in '70:
No blood for oil. Iraq is Arabic for Vietnam.
Except now what hair we have is gray or dyed,
showing even we are surrendering to time.
Some of the younger ones wield babies—
sure-fire arms for claiming the high ground.
One guy's stuffed himself into his old
Army field jacket: another veteran for peace.
But the folks across the street chanting
support our troops don't get his point.
And in case we don't get theirs, our mayor
crosses over to parade his bass drum belly
and waving flag before us.

My son died for you guys,
one woman screams
from her car window.
I want to stop her, sit her down,
tell her my son is out there somewhere
in Iraq, Afghanistan, or Jordan.
He can't tell me. But now it's me
behind the wheel, anger pressing
hard on my heart's accelerator,
and my son is never coming back.
If I had a gun, I'd shoot right through
their signs and hope to God a few
of them went down. When I screech
into my driveway, I lay my head down
on the wheel, let sobbing take my body.

Then I'm back, holding a sign
as subtle as a sawed-off shotgun.
When the words I need to explain
my standing here to her are too many
and too quiet to appear on any sign.
Words that hold no weapons,
wear no armor. Or they're written
on the side I'm staring into—
the blank side, the side that listens.

Van Gogh's Pieta

"In a picture I want to say something comforting."
—Van Gogh

More *pas de deux* than *pieta*,
they hold the pose
ancient as the repertoire
of son and mother.

Limp as any fish, he flops
into the waiting blue
waves of her raiment,
his chest green, gold,
cerise—a rippled sunset.

The sad part is how far
he is beyond her comfort.
Even if he could feel
the cool cave of her body,
dip his hand into the tonic
of her sorrow, the punctured
palm would come up empty.

I came to the exhibit expecting
the dark shudder of crows' wings,
an orange sun that shows no mercy,
an indigo so deep I could stop seeing
my own grown son's face twisted
in the turbulence I drown in.

All I want to do now
is fall back into the arms
of a child's faith, let myself
be lulled past the horizon
by a sunset so beautiful
it must be true.

The Way to Forgiveness

is a long trudge through deep snow
back to the orange plastic chair
in the surgery waiting room where
the phone finally rings, and it's
the doctor with the wrong news,
hanging up before you can recover
enough to ask questions. Out the window
you see him striding to his car
and bolt out the door, calling his name.
He doesn't want to stop, doesn't turn
until you yell again, running to catch up.

Who's going to tell the man you've loved
for thirty years that he's not in the lucky
75% whose cancer hasn't spread
beyond the bladder's borders?
You can, I suppose, he says, like a boy
caught in a cowardly act, no
intention of repenting as he opens
the door to his sleek getaway car.

And now you're in the room waiting
for your husband to wake full of hope,
knowing you must break the news,
and when he wants to ask what
it means, he'll be shocked that the man—
so friendly last week in his office,
giving a jovial punch to his shoulder—
hasn't stayed to give him the prognosis.

But five years is too long to wait
for forgiveness to come on its own
like Spring and chip the crusted ice
around your heart. It's up to you
to slog through your anger, your
resistance, to slip and cut your knees
while tears freeze on your cheeks.

To warm yourself with maybes—
like maybe he wanted too badly
to be able to say the happy words
you both had waited for, or maybe
he couldn't be strong like you,
closing your eyes now, returning
to the room where your beloved lies
beneath a sheet like the blanket of snow
that will cover him in a few months.
Now open your eyes and write
the poem to save you from the cold.

I Call to You from Time

From a season of sparrows
grateful for seed, from a morning
when watching their feeding
is all the prayer I have in me.

This is the tithing I offer—
this moment, tiny as the millet seed
one bird lifts in her perfect beak.
I swear she looks straight at me
as, in a gesture like my head
tilting back to take the wine,
she swallows.

O God, never stop
feeding me these moments.
Keep tearing through the blue
curtain of eternity to find me
here, behind the kitchen window,
drinking my coffee, doing Time.

If She Could

> from the painting by Fra Angelico and helper,
> in Cell 8, the Cloister of San Marco

Of course, she wants to believe
what the angel perching on the edge
of the sarcophagus is saying.

But first let her lean into the darkness,
shading her eyes from the glare above.
Let her search for the body we both loved.

Any moment she will give up,
see the angel pointing to the gleaming
bubble overhead where he is floating.

Angelico, I hear what you are saying.
I know sooner or later she must look up.
But right now leave her to her human grieving.

Let choirs and priests in some distant basilica rejoice.
I'll stay here with her, gripping
the marble's cold lip till it warms us.

Our Lady Releasing Her Sorrow

from the bulto *painting by Carol Mothner*

One palm lies in the other,
cups the dove-shaped space
where, only a wing-stroke ago,
sorrow rested so close
beneath her breast
its fluttering nearly
erased her heartbeat.

Although it's flown away,
her arms have held this pose
for centuries and can't
remember any other mission,
any more than her scalp
recalls a time it didn't sting
with this tiara of gold tears.

But now, like some wise ghost,
her shadow lifts its skirt
and swivels toward the future.
Any moment she will wake
from wood, drop the emptiness
that holds her still
and follow.

Echo, Late Winter

on a line from a rabbi's prayer in a Hasidic tale

Lord, let this world continue one more day
if you must as grief gnaws at our bones
and snow drifts over us in endless waves.

In one way or another we're all strays.
Let starving dogs have one more night to roam.
Lord, let this world continue one more day.

Perhaps a day for sniffing at the graves
where lie our abandoned prayers and poems
buried by the snow in endless waves.

A day of pawing through what can't be saved,
to lose claws digging to an ancient home.
Lord, let this world continue one more day.

Let us create a keening in our cave,
howl for every creature we have known
buried by the snow in endless waves.

Let our warm hands give shape to frozen clay—
a beautiful container for our moans.
Lord, let this world continue one more day
as snow drifts over us in endless waves.

Rebirth

For months we sisters prayed—
    not for the 18-year-old-boy
    to crash his car—
for a healthy lung to find our sister.
She packed a suitcase as in the weeks
before each daughter's birth, and when
one daughter called to say our sister
got the call and was driving to the hospital,
we waited the whole night through,
the way we had in semi-gloom
of labor rooms for the dawning
of our babies' heads. And when we knew
she'd made it, we wanted to call
friends and proclaim: *It's a sister!*

His other lung went to another woman,
and they were harvesting his heart and liver
for two others. I couldn't stop my brain
returning to him—a young man driving along
on a sunny day who'd suddenly arrived
at being called *the donor*. I kept seeing a strange
last supper table where he played host,
offering the bounty of his body.

Off the ventilator, on her feet in record time,
our sister's recovery is called *miraculous.*
We savor that morsel on our tongues,
repeating it to all we know who need
such a story. Which, it turns out, is everyone.

Not to mention the miracle of the donor's *yes*
and hers colliding, making their pact with life.
Still, some traitor in my heart keeps hissing:
*why should she have had the miracle
and not that guy?* Of course,
the answer is *because I love her.*

She says that in the x-rays
her new lung is a white feather,
and I believe I know the bird who dropped it—
isn't it the holy spirit in a holding pattern,
bright flickering above each sacred moment,
wings spread wide over us all,
whether or not we see it?

Lenten Practice as the Climate Changes

You can take it as a sign of grace—
indigo wings hovering above the birdhouses
you haven't cleaned yet, it's so early.

But even as you gather bucket, screwdriver
and scraper for this most hopeful duty,
even as bluebird, gold crocus, and the screech

of redwings crack the world's gray shell,
you know you shouldn't shout hallelujah
at this premature rebirth. Yet

as the seasons swing out of their senses,
you practice this small ritual of preparation,
pry open the wooden door and dismantle

last year's weave—grass, twigs, feathers—
leave your prayer of nothing
to welcome the wings that are coming.

Grace

from the colorized photograph by Ernest Enstrom

No doubt you'd recognize this old gentleman.
He hangs above many a faithful table,
his creased forehead leaning into the gnarled
nest of folded fingers, grateful for the crumbs of life—
a humble loaf, a bowl of soup waiting near his elbows,
light seeping from an unknown source above him.

When my son found him a few days before Christmas,
propped against the dumpster outside the apartment
he rarely leaves, he wondered how anyone could
abandon him there and brought him inside,
happy to offer him *a proper home.*

That's how my son is, you see—
recognizing a life where others see an object.
Maybe he gets it from his crazy mother
who believes God leaves us such windows.
Or maybe it's this season when we yearn
to shelter whatever comes knocking
in whatever shape it appears.

Screen Saver

If I'm not quick enough with word or phrase,
the birds of Sanibel Island begin appearing,
and once again I'm kayaking between them,
glad to be diverted from the muddy slough I'm stuck in.

Gliding down the jade tunnel of mangroves,
I catch the cormorant hanging out his wings to dry,
swiveling on his black toes to follow my movement.

Around the bend the snowy egret stands erect and still,
sentinel guarding an ancient secret. And here
comes the green heron, offering her single eye to mine.

If I glance behind them, I find the birds of winter
visiting my feeder, one after another like dancers
flitting from behind the arbor vitae curtain for their solos.

I don't see them composing nests from the old year's bones.
But I have an idea how it goes.
For the same complicated need to make something
new from twigs and scraps
is always washing over me like spring.

This afternoon, though, each bird's beauty
is sufficient to convince me to lay down
my paddle, all my striving, and enter
the silence that surrounds them.

Glory to the Chickadee, Cardinal,
and Junco, as it was in the beginning,
is now, and ever shall be,
world without words.
Amen.

Our Lady of the Rest Stop

Last time I saw her—no kidding—
she was descending from a beat-up
Winnebago in the Sandhills just north
of Hyannis, Nebraska, wearing blue,
like always, except now
it's a wind-bleached denim sundress.

And this time there's no halo
except around everything
in her vicinity: the kids pulling fish
from the river, the fish themselves—
their fins like pearly wings—
the vials of wild plum wine
someone has left in the shallows,
cooling. The cooing pair
of doves pecking at pebbles.

And when she shakes your hand
it too starts glowing, not
so you can see it, but so you know
finally how good it is
to have a palm and fingers.
And all you want to do is
spread that sheen on everything
you can get your hands on,

to make it feel
like it's just been washed
in brightest water
as though it is a fish
that dreamed itself
into an angel.

Prayer Flags

I see now why each line of wash
in a backyard makes me want to drop
down on my knees, that I am witnessing
the prayer of t-shirts, blue jeans, sheets
and underwear—the prayer flapping
below terra cotta rooftops in Siena
repeated in the same tongue right here
in Tioga County, Pennsylvania.

Don't tell me those women don't know
they are praying. Have you ever
watched even a busy woman hanging
out the holy ghosts of her family?
Seen her stand there afterwards,
her empty basket resting like a child
on her cocked hip, as she adored
the spirit of the wind tossing them
into the deep blue mind of heaven?

Even a grieving woman feels her feet
lift from the earth when the breeze
kicks up the ankles of her drying khakis,
feels her shoulders sprouting wings
as her blouse takes flight. I don't know
if she is grateful as she clips each
garment to her line, or if each one
bodies forth a precious worry.
Maybe her clothesline is one long wail.

But watch her hours later
when she goes to bring her wash in,
leaning into the warm scent of sun
woven with birdsong, closing her eyes
for just a second as she guesses
this must be how God smells,
pulling each piece into an embrace
of folding, settling it in her basket,
and giving the whole stack a final pat.

Junction

from the woodcut/monoprint by Dan Welden

Any room can be a junction,
even if no artist comes along
to paint it, even with no rectangle
etched into the concrete
and brushed a dirty white
to let the light in.

Any room can be the place
the light ignites inside you,
and though you might be strung
across the canvas in a hammock,
you can rise up from the bondage
you no longer have a use for.

Turn your head.
See these splotches daubed
over what might be portholes?
Even if you can't see

through them to an empty canvas,
in your pocket sleeps a tube of color.
Here's this brush.
Now wake up.
Here's this new light.

www.ingramcontent.com/pod-product-compliance
Lightning Source LLC
Chambersburg PA
CBHW071315110426
42743CB00042B/2242